The Seven Sorrows of the Virgin Mary with the Holy Pope John Paul II

Table of Contents

1- Introduction

2- Recommendation

3- Reflections with each pain of the Virgin Mary in the Holy Way of the Cross with John Paul II.

4- Holy Rosary

Introduction

In this book you will find reflections through prayers of the seven sorrows of the Virgin Mary and how John Paul II taught us through his life and his work, how we must transform painful experiences into wisdom, to give utility of change to our life and direct it towards the refuge of the giver of absolute truth, of the only one who can give real and eternal happiness by inviting us to be spiritual soldiers, because although it causes pain the mission of helping the deviant neighbor to get back on track in the real love of God is worth it, since the reward is gratifying.

Recommendation

It is recommended to periodically attend the Holy Eucharist, try to realize the commandments of the church and put into practice the gifts of the holy spirit, performing charitable works and preaching the word of our beloved father.

Prayer for every day

Blessed, man of impeccable virtue, your dear John Paul who went through daring throughout your life, to remind your neighbor of the message that I had forgotten from the creator, today I approach you to thank you for that beautiful mission, I thank you because your task of guiding hearts so that they were transformed constantly seeking to fulfill the will of the creator for their lives and the truth that comes from our beloved father, I beg you honorable gentleman to accompany me in the intimacy of my heart to have a communion with my creator and to express to him my repentance for my sins, so that his infinite mercy may exonerate me from all guilt, and I may commit myself to analyze every step that comes into my existence so as not to make mistakes again, nor actions that put my salvation and my eternal life under his shelter at risk.

Read Psalm 91

Prayer remembering the first sorrow of the Virgin Mary in simeon's prophecy

Beloved Mary, your human being who never questioned the will of the creator, and you perfectly fulfilled your mission of being the mother of the savior, I understand your pain as a mother to know the martyrdoms that your beloved son would suffer for the salvation of the sins of humanity, your faithful companion and guide of John Paul II in all his pilgrimages through the world you whispered wisdom to guide everyone who was immersed in the forest of easy path of spiritual lie, regaining sight and returning to the path although difficult that leads them to the forest of spiritual truth, St. Simeon prophesied to the Virgin Mary the pain that would come to her life and yet our mother did not decline in her battle because she knew that after that pain great things would come for humanity, allows every painful experience through which I go through my destiny dear John Paul second to place it in the hands of God since he will soon expel pain from me, he will transform it into wisdom to manage my destiny, so that my daily life is to his liking and my existence is not lost and on the contrary I can with the wisdom of what I have learned through the present pain fulfill his will for the good of humanity.

Read Luke 22:22-35

Prayer remembering the flight to Egypt of our Virgin Mary praying to our holy Pope John Paul II.

Beloved John Paul second, you who despite the dangers you went through in your earthly journey, never declined before your service, before the work of bringing peace, love, understanding in every corner where you were called, your mind and heart through constant prayer, the voice of the creator guided the threads of your steps, taking you to places where they should know of the water that satisfies spiritual thirst, just as the angel whispered in dreams to Joseph to leave for Egypt to save the savior's life, so they were revealed to you how you should guide the church to fulfill the will of God, likewise through prayer I guided you to be a missionary and a wise preacher, correct, polishing the qualities of the church and oppressing its defects, in the same way I beg you dear holy pope, that my life be guided to make the best decisions in my life, so that I can discern the good from the bad, what builds and what destroys, so that I can become like you a worthy soldier of Christ, capable of giving return to the light of God to every neighbor lost in the lies that the present world delivers and help them to find their salvation, making them worthy of the blessings of the beloved father, so that at the end of my days like you and our virgin Mary may enjoy the eternal warm love of one who created all that exists

Read Matthew 2:13-15.

Prayer for John Paul II reflecting on the third sorrow of our Virgin Mary when the beloved Jesus was lost in the temple.

Your dear friend, honorable gentleman, who renounced himself to be a soldier of Christ and take his word to every corner of the earth, I thank you because your germine seed in many hearts including mine, the same feeling that the Virgin Mary lived when she lost her son, is lived daily by our creator with all the sheep of his flock lost, you were an excellent shepherd since through you the beloved heavenly father was able to caress again with his pure love several of his beloved children, including myself, thank you dear John Paul ii because with your example of life you made me admire you wanting to clean my heart, self-heal me of all pain, self-forgiving me for every mistake made, reborn again in faith, strengthening my hope, committed to serving everyone who is in darkness consciously or unconsciously as you did in earthly life or as you do now that you enjoy the crown of a saint

Read Luke, 2:41-51

Prayer or reflection of the encounter of the Virgin Mary with Jesus on the way to Calvary with John Paul II

Beloved John Paul SECOND, you always reminded the faithful of the church of the painful task of our beloved Jesus, but at the same time you accompanied our mother Mary in the pain that she had to live when seeing her son martyred, our creator every day feels pain to see how humanity is being lost by the ambition of the material, because first build goods and if you have time build your spirit, guide me so that my greatest desire is to meet my beloved heavenly father every day of my existence, since next to my creator all bliss will come if it is deserved, help me to sow the seed in rebellious hearts so that in them germinate the nourishing fruit of the creator so that when our creator returns again I did not ratify his pain of seeing humanity lost in the lies that the owner of darkness has given, I know that by committing myself to the service of God I will have painful experiences as the Virgin Mary had, but they will make me wise and build my spirit, I know that the effort will lead me to an eternal reward, the experience that causes pain today, it can be the one that gives wisdom and strength to face battles in posterity, your beloved john Paul II you were a living example that the pain of today makes you wiser in tomorrow, you who suffered from attacks and was more the pain of your heart than that of your body, seeing that humanity insists on questioning the will and commands of those who created them, help me to make myself like you and the Virgin Mary, capable of transforming pain into virtue, into teaching for others so that they become aware that nothing in the universe succeeds if it departs from the giver of existence itself.

Read Lam 1,12

Reflection on the death of Christ on the cross with John Paul II

Beloved John Paul II, I thank the beloved creator father who gave the mission to you, which you fulfilled successfully and thousands on earth today live a spiritual ecstasy that gives them incalculable joy and happiness, allows them to be aware that to have that salvation and that communion with God it was necessary for him to give his beloved son , although he cared about the pain of his beloved mother, he allowed him to feel it and that made our mother Maria more perfect, more aware of the human pain caused by the wounds sent by the devil himself to destroy his creation, and today our beloved virgin Mary fights so that humanity is not lost and returns to the arms of the creator, I beg you dear gentleman john paul second, that you help me in this breakdown, in this problem that causes me pain, that takes me along the paths of anxiety, fear or uncertainty that your light and that of my divine mother take me to the place where I will solve my problem or bring to me the person who will extend my hand, I know that you with the Blessed Virgin understand what I feel now and that makes them have great piety, if it is your will to extend your hand and heal everything that causes anxiety so that I can calmly exercise the mission that the creator has for my existence so that he sows through me the seed of good so that his will may be done before the existing, do not let him forget the pain of the Virgin Mary when she sees her beloved son on the cross since that experience makes it conscious that I am not alone in the spiritual struggle, and if I place my burden in her hands it will not become so heavy and impossible to bear and at some point when she understands the lesson given it will be the burden removed and I will be able to enjoy the beatitudes that the creator has. for me, although my existence alone is a sign of his infinite love and infinite mercy.

Read John 19-17-39

Reflection when the Virgin Mary lived the descent of her beloved son from the cross and placed in her arms

Blessed John Paul II, may the pride of my heart be separated and be aware that knowing the word of our Lord I make bad decisions which led me to pain, anguish, insecurity of everyday life, that although the world offers solutions to achieve happiness, they are weak since they are not spiritual but based on money, in the material, solutions that come disguised as ight but are coming from the darkness, but you, the right hand of the creator on earth, reminded me through the pain he felt of the Virgin Mary when he saw his son come down from that torture that lived on the cross, which is at that moment where 1e gives me salvation, It reminds me of his death and the pain of my mother the Virgin Mary, that it is never too late to have intimacy with my heavenly father and to commit myself with his help to cleanse my soul, my heart, my very essence, so that he may become an instrument as you were your beloved John Paul II, and I can after my pain of soul, know the real and true happiness, the same that the Virgin Mary lives eternally, which I managed to obtain by doing the will of God without questioning it, and she does not care about the pain of a mother, to see her son persecuted, questioned, martyred, never gave up despite her brokenness because she had the certainty that everything related to her son was the absolute truth, allow my free will to give it to God as your John Paul II did, to do

wonders in me as he does in the Virgin Mary through time and
as he did with you in the period you sat on the highest throne
of the church and do them today through miracles even
though you are already under his warm eternal shelter.

Read verse John 18-38

Reflection when our beloved Jesus is buried

Beloved John Paul II, dear friend, it is painful to see for the
last time a loved one, the pain that the Virgin Mary felt when
she saw her adored son for the last time, but her heart had
faith that she would never stop feeling her love, that her
relationship would not end when she saw him in the tomb, that
her communion with the creator and her spiritual ecstasy
would continue eternally, your dear john paul ii taught us
throughout your work as high priest that we must kill the
wrong person of the past and give birth or resurrection to a
new being, and that can only be achieved by the hand of God,
since he has the power to do so as long as we place our free
will at his disposal, the virgin Mary tired of feeling pain never
renounced it, she lived with courage her trials, her pain and her
soul was perfected so much that Through time today she
enjoys heavenly purity and is seated on the throne that extends
truth and love, allows her to discern, understand the life lesson
that I have to live Through of the experience that I am living,
because this experience is only a process like the caterpillar that
must wait to become a butterfly, I beg you dear friend to
accompany me in the process of killing the being that is in the
darkness to the being that does not want the vision of his soul
to return and can be reborn in me the one who wishes to live

in spirit without desiring the spiritual life accompany me to live my to awaken, to become the butterfly of light, to understand my prose of change as the Virgin Mary lives it, to understand that birds pain forges the best swords, the best spiritual armor.

Read Luke 23:53-54

HOLY ROSARY

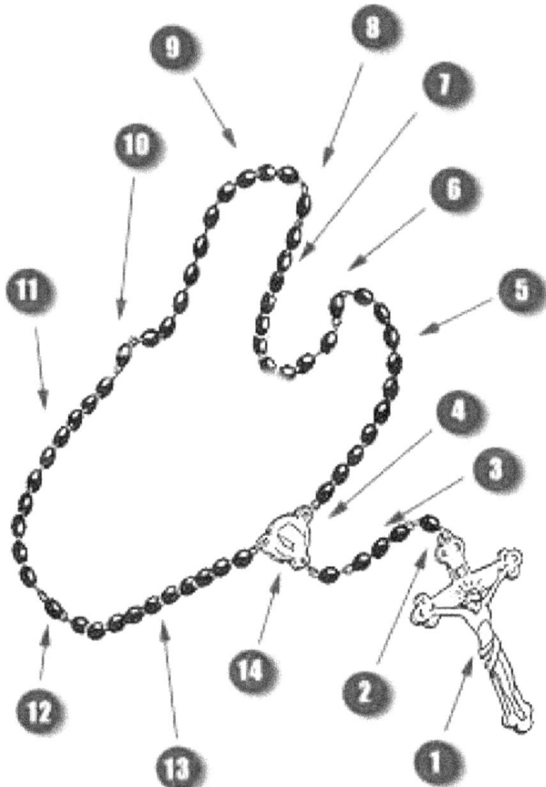

1- PERSIGNATION
2- THE CREED
3- FIRST SPHERE: THE HAIL QUEEN AND
MOTHER, SECOND SPHERE: THE GLORY OF
MASS, THIRD SPHERE: THE I CONFESS, FOURTH
SPHERE: PSALM 91

4- FIRST INTENTION

Dear John Paul ii, to you I come with my soul despondent of pain for all the experiences lived in life, equal to the pain that our mother Maria felt, may your holy light help me to cleanse my heart, my soul, to help me heal it so that it is worthy that in it the holy spirit dwells so that its gifts germinate in me and I can use them for my benefit and as you did your that you placed them at the service of others.

5- Ten Saint Marys, two our fathers, two glory to the father.

6- SECOND INTENTION

Dear John Paul II, may my heart flee before the dark things, before the things that destroy the spiritual seeds, may I flee like Mary and Jose before the dangers that the child god ran because of the acts of the devil so that he did not fulfill the mission of the salvation of humanity, that my soul does not get lost and knows how to flee that knows how to dodge the the darts that the devil sends me so that in me the will of my creator is not done, be your protective shield against these attacks and expel every dark larva that wants to eat away at my existence, guide me to make as you an impeccable missionary, a brave soldier to help others to get out of the mud Of the lying happiness that gives the spirit of darkness through the material things that understand the importance of strengthening the soul with the things of the creator.

7- Ten Saint Marys, two our fathers, two glory to the father.

8- TERECERA INTENTION

Blessed and honest man, may your light, if it is your will and with the permission of the creator, be poured out on me so that you may bless all the provisions that come to my table, fruit of the arduous and honest work, that my happiness is not in accumulating goods, that my happiness is in accumulating spiritual goods but that they are not saved inside me but that I can like you spread them, teach them to those who lack intelligence before the things of God, so that they do not make mistakes and sin by ignorance that can share them and are useful to quench the thirst of everyone who lacks it and as well as your place a grain of sand so that humanity is on its way to having again a harmonious and constant communion with the creator.

9- Ten Saint Marys, two our fathers, two glory to the father.

10-   FOURTH INTENTION

Loved by multitudes, may your holy light always accompany us, may your holy light as it falls on me and help me to forgive, to reconcile with myself and with my neighbor and whispers wisdom to me to handle the threads of my destiny, if it is your will also be for my family for each member of it, I ask you dear john paul second that you expel from his side every chain of destructive curse, so that they can have prosperity given by the creator, heal my family and that their priority is always to congregate to boast of the things of the creator that not only remain in noun but in verb as you did your dear brother.

11-   Ten Saint Mary, two our fathers, two glory the father.

12-	FIFTH INTENTION

Dear John Paul, may my life value every pain of our mother Mary when she lived the Way of the Cross that her beloved son suffered for our salvation and understand the lesson that God wants to give us with the life experience that our mother had to go through, that my life does not waste my existence, her sacrifice and my life, that my actions polish my spirit even if they are painful. May it be for God and for the Virgin Mary a fine tool as you are who want to use it eternally for the harmony between the divine and the human whose tool is sharp in the face of the things of evil, and after the wounds it causes by telling the absolute truth that comes from God comes an impeccable spiritual healing for all those who deviated from the path because of the lies of the evil one.

13-	Ten Saint Marys, two our fathers, two glory to the father.

14-   Final prayer.

Dear John Paul II, just as you visited several places on earth I beg you to come and visit my home, my chambers, my family that your holy energy restores all those that are damaged with the help of our Lord Jesus Christ, that everything that is damaged in our family be replaced by the things of the creator and my family nucleus become reformers of hearts, in spirit reformers that mankind may scale up and fully fulfill the commandment to love one another as his holy son taught us.

POSDATA: It is recommended to offer a Mass for all the saints in gratitude for all the favors received.